NICOLE DARKO

I0171465

LIGHT OFF

A Call to Illuminate the World

HONEY PRESS

Copyright © 2015 Nicole Darko

All rights reserved.

Cover Design: Charis Lema

ISBN: 0692550887
ISBN-13: 9780692550885

Praise for LIGHT OFF

After reading Light Off, you will be informed, enlightened, but more importantly strongly challenged as a believer to be the "light" of Christ shining in "darkness." Although, we assume to understand Jesus' message and mandate to be the "light of the world," Light Off provides us with a different perspective. It reminds us that it is out of the darkness that light shines. I sense the book to be the "Pulse" of Christ and the "Heartbeat" of the Father.

-Apostle William T. Ford, Sr., Senior Pastor,
Kingdom Impact Global Ministries

"Light Off is in one word, BRILLIANT! It provides a refreshing awakening to the true heart of God for mankind. Nicole has in a few words rekindled the fire in our hearts to be a light in a dark world and never go out. The Light On movement will be one of many tools that God will use to reach the world."

-Charles Bloom, Senior Pastor,
Kingdom Minded Ministries

"Even after 20 years of on-the-field Missions experience, I found Light Off to be not only an encouragement for seasoned missionaries but an inspiration to those considering cross-cultural service. The authentic passion to see The Gospel light-up places that have been dark for far too long becomes contagious within these pages. I strongly recommend Light Off to be necessary reading for any short-term team preparing for ministry, as well as, The Body of Christ at large. And it is my prayer that "Light On" becomes the catalyst for a global movement...Light Off is a bright idea."

-Rev. Keith W. Jaggers, President,
Missionaries On Special Assignment

"The initial excitement of finally embarking on a long awaited life's journey soon turned to trepidation, right before the greatest spiritual, eye-opening revelation Nicole Darko ever had. Light Off unfolds this revelation and helps us better understand how Believers can illuminate the dark places. A MUST read for the lighted soul!"

-Raul Wallace, Assistant Pastor,
Kingdom Impact Global Ministries

"Nicole's honest summary of their experience in Ghana portrays the reality that most missionaries grow to see: we go to serve, but perhaps the greatest work God does is the work He does in us as we obey His command. We go to impact; we become the one impacted. Her open portrayal of 'light off' in Ghana and the application to a world in spiritual darkness is one example of God's good work in His children. May we listen with our hearts, and learn."

-Dr. Joe Hale, President,
Network of International Christian Schools

This book is dedicated to the 1.2 billion people across the globe who still do not have access to electricity and to the 26.4 million Ghanaians who coined the term "light off" to explain the inconsistent supply of electricity to their great nation.[i]

CONTENTS

Acknowledgments

Holy Spirit, your friendship and guidance are incomparable.

Prince, your name falls short in revealing your true nature, for you are my king, second only to the King of Kings.

David and Victoria, what incredible tutors you have been and continue to be as I seek to parent you in the fear and admonition of the Lord.

Daddy, Mama, Barbara, and Angela, your examples of perseverance and expressions of unconditional love have given me an unshakeable foundation.

Apostle William T. Ford, Sr., thank you for your compassionate shepherding of God's flock and for the unparalleled wisdom and prophetic insight that you freely share with the sheep.

Preface

If you have grown up in a Western country like me, then you are probably unfamiliar with the phrase "light off" or the local Ghanaian saying *dumsor, dumsor*, which means "on and off, on and off." I became acquainted with this phrase when my family and I, in obedience to God's call, packed our bags and moved from our comfortable suburban life in Fayetteville, North Carolina, to my husband's native land of Ghana, located in West Africa. This book was birthed out of my experiences in living without consistent electricity for three years and what the Lord taught me through the process. It is my prayer that the lessons in this book will help each of us become the light in places that remain dark, both naturally and spiritually.

Chapter

"While I am in the world, I am the Light of the world."

—John 9:5 (NASB)

Let me begin by saying that despite my sincere love for God and passion for missions, I am an American who grew up in a middle-class family; therefore, my experiences with Ghana's electricity crisis are colored by this privileged Western lens. Although I began serving God through short-term missions at the age of nineteen, I really didn't understand the vast differences that were inherent in long-term missions. I readily accepted the challenges of living temporarily in a developing country, and I assumed that my previous experience had prepared me to face those challenges for the long term.

Unfortunately, I was sorely mistaken, and my missionary ideals came crumbling down.

I knew that despite my prior short-term mission's experience, moving to a foreign country permanently with two small children would be a new experience for me. So, before we officially relocated with our children (ages seven and four), like any good parent, I researched as much as I could about our new home. I became an expert about things like malaria prevention and ended up buying every citronella candle, arm band, and sticker that I could find. I googled popular restaurants that serve American food and was pleasantly surprised to discover that there was a KFC in my city (now there are three!).

We were moving to Ghana in part to serve as missionary teachers at one of the international Christian schools in the city. So while we were prepared to live in a mud hut and hunt and gather our food, we were pleasantly surprised to be living in the capital city, located in a very upscale part of town.

Teaching in a Christian school where students arrive in Range Rovers and Mercedes Benz made our "sacrifice" to move thousands of miles across the globe feel more like a windfall and less like a sacrifice. This, in part, made the adjustment of "carrying my cross" harder to accept because, initially, it didn't seem like a cross at all.[2] Nevertheless, I e-mailed current teachers at the school and continued to ask questions that my Internet searches had failed to answer. Again, to my delight, I was inundated with responses telling me places to get my hair relaxed, places to take the children on the weekends, and the best places to shop.

In the days leading up to our departure, I asked a future colleague what they found to be the most difficult part about living in Ghana, and their response was simply this: "light off." At that time, those two words meant very little to me because a lack of electricity for limited amounts of time didn't seem like it would be too difficult. After all, we could be living in a village where there was no electricity at all. Furthermore, having lived in the South for most of my life, I was accustomed to the summer thunderstorm that temporarily knocked out electricity, and I often enjoyed the cool breeze and eerie quiet that followed. Nevertheless, I tried to prepare myself for the times when we would be without lights by stocking up on solar-powered lamps, battery-operated fans, and personalized flashlights for everyone.

We arrived in Ghana toward the end of July and were welcomed by cool temperatures and constant electricity. Our first experience with "light off" came about three weeks after our arrival, and I was pleasantly surprised by how unaffected we all were, especially the children. That first time, the lights were off for about four or five hours, and it was midafternoon, so we were virtually unfazed. I thought about my colleague's response and chalked up her difficulties in adjusting to infrequent electricity to a temperament difference. Little did I know how those two words, "light off," would stretch my attitude, patience, and faith over the next three years.

Chapter

"So Jesus said to them, 'For a little while longer the light is among you. Walk while you have the light, so that darkness will not overtake you; he who walks in the darkness does not know where he goes.'"

—John 12:35 (NASB)

Led by the late Kwame Nkrumah, Ghana positioned itself early on as a leading African nation by being the first sub-Saharan country to establish true democracy on the continent. The land is rich in natural resources such as cocoa, gold, bauxite, timber, and now oil. Despite these God-given riches, Ghana's leaders, like many African nations, have failed to appropriate the funds generated from these resources to address the infrastructural needs of the country. Ghana Grid Company, or GridCo, and the Volta

River Authority are tasked with transmitting electricity across the nation. The Northern Electricity Distribution Company and the Electricity Company of Ghana (ECG), both government-owned entities, are solely responsible for selling electricity to Ghana's twenty-six million citizens.[3] Since our arrival, promises of improved transmission and distribution have not materialized due to alleged mismanagement, antiquated machinery, and increasing demand.

After about three months of living in our new home, the excitement had worn off and frustration had set in. My *laissez-faire* attitude had been replaced with impatience, annoyance, and anger.[4] Initially, the lights were off for a couple of hours a few days a week, but as time progressed we found ourselves without electricity for twelve hours a day, every day. As difficult as this was to adjust to, what sent me over the edge was when our twelve hours of darkness were extended to eighteen and then twenty hours. Not only were we virtually in the dark most evenings, but we were also in the heat. The cool temperatures in July when we arrived soon gave way to hot, thick air which is characteristic of the dry season. The phrase "light off" is a bit misleading because it fails to communicate that "light off" also means "air conditioner off," "fan off," and "refrigerator off." To bring some perspective to the situation, Ghana is located a few degrees north of the equator, and no electricity for extended amounts of time meant "life off" for me.

I prayed for patience, quoted scripture, and encouraged the children to be grateful for the times when we had some electricity. It was difficult because for the first two years, we did not have a car nor the means to purchase one on our missionary salaries. Initially, we embraced the adventure of walking down dirt roads, greeting our neighbors, and watching the occasional goat, sheep, or chicken cross our paths. These walks made us feel like we were true missionaries living the missionary dream and provided us with great photos to send back home to our supporters—until the novelty wore off. "Light off" didn't just affect us at home; the lack of electricity at work exacerbated our discontentment.

After walking for twenty minutes in the thick, damp morning air, sometimes we would arrive at work only to discover that the generator was broken. This news was as if someone had heaped coals upon our heads. A lack of electricity at work meant that we would spend eight hours in a hot five-story building with no printing, photocopying, or Internet capabilities. All the while we felt responsible for encouraging students and colleagues to choose joy in the midst of this situation. After all, that was the reason that we left our home, cars, and constant electricity in America, wasn't it?

Those days were especially difficult because we had to walk back home to a stifling hot and humid house, only to discover that our food in the refrigerator had spoiled due to the extended power outages. Unsure as to whether the lights would return before sundown, which is around 6:00 p.m. year round (unlike the summer months in the United States), we would rush to complete homework, cook dinner, wash dishes, take baths, make lunches for the next day, and iron clothes because without the sun there was no light. Once the sun would set and the lights did not return, we would all gather in one room, make pallets on the floor (because it was the coolest place in the house), and go to bed, sometimes even before 7:00 p.m. We were forced to make decisions like whether to suffocate from the sweltering heat or open the windows and be swarmed by blood-sucking mosquitos. Due to my extensive research about malaria, we initially opted for option one, but as twelve-hour evenings became more and more frequent, we swung open our windows and attempted to fall asleep to the low whine of dozens of mosquitos' wings buzzing in our ears. Needless to say, when we awoke most mornings, we were covered with bites in various places.

At the height of the energy crisis, ECG published a schedule of outages and informed customers what time and on which days outages would occur. Despite my sheer disgust at the situation, I was thankful to have a schedule to know when I could iron all of the clothes for the week, when I could have hot water for a bath, and when I could have a night alone with my husband (the children refused to sleep in their own rooms when the electricity was off). Unfortunately, ECG did not follow the published schedule, and on some days that we were supposed to have electricity, we were sitting in the dark. Like any red-blooded American, I called ECG and asked why the electricity wasn't on despite having been off for our allotted time. I demanded answers, but the gravity of the situation was met with indolence.

The lack of urgency on the part of the operator and the repeated empty promises pushed me over the edge, and I cried out to God. All of the prayers for patience and maintaining a proper attitude were replaced by an all-out rant. I proceeded to remind God how I left everything in America to come to Ghana in obedience to His will. I jogged His memory about being willing to bring my seven-year-old and four-year-old to a place that few people would have faith enough to bring their children. I pulled the stewardship card and told Him how we were continually paying high electricity bills when we barely had electricity. I explained how we were wasting money buying groceries, only to have to throw them away because they were spoiled due to the lack of refrigeration. Exhausted from my cacophony of words that dripped with self-righteousness, I was finally empty and sat quietly in the dark. After some time, I distinctly remember the Holy Spirit asking me, "Why are you so frustrated?"

Why am I so frustrated? Isn't that just like God to ask you a question when you want answers? I said, "I'm frustrated because the sole reason that ECG exists is to provide electricity to the citizens of Ghana, and they can't do that one thing."

What the Holy Spirit said next revolutionized my life and became the catalyst for this book. He said, "The same frustration that you feel toward ECG is equivalent to the frustration that those who sit in darkness feel as they wait for the manifestation of those whom I called to be the light of the world. As a Christian, your sole reason for existing is to be the light, and like ECG you make excuses as to why you can't shine in dark places."

Upon hearing these words from the Lord, I repented. I confessed my self-centeredness and my preoccupation with "me" and "mine." I realized that although my mission field looked different from what I expected, the call to sacrifice was the same. Had I been living in a village with no electricity or running water, I would've been content knowing that denying myself was a part of the cost of following Christ. Somehow working in a school with affluent students located in a wealthy part of town clouded my perspective and caused me to lose sight of the mission. I had fallen prey to the brand of Christianity that desires to reign with Christ but refuses to suffer with Him.

We moved to Ghana because God called us to be a light, but somehow I got sidetracked and unknowingly became a part of the spiritual phenomenon called "light off." I don't believe that I am the only one, and so I asked the Holy Spirit how this happened and what the remedy was for the problem. What He shared with me is contained in the following chapters.

Chapter

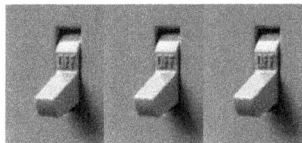

"You are the light of the world."

—Matthew 5:14 (NASB)

Over the next few days, I began analyzing
Matthew 5:14 and tried to discover what it truly
means to be the light of the world. The first thing that
I noticed about this verse was that when Jesus says,
"You are the light of the world," He has revealed the
mission, the call, and the purpose for all those who
place their trust in Him. Oftentimes, as Christians, we
are in search of our calling, our destiny, and our
purpose. We want God to speak to us in bold, audible
terms, but He has already revealed the call of every
believer in this one verse. Jesus unpacks this
revelation by carefully choosing seven words that on

the surface seem benign but in truth are life changing.

The verse begins with the pronoun "you," which indicates that Jesus is speaking to a specific audience and that His message is especially for them. Jesus could've said, "My disciples" or "My followers," but instead He chose the word "you." This indicates that the substance of His message was for everyone who was presently listening to Him. This is important because we often think that God is talking to other people instead of clearly discerning that His "you" means "us." Somehow we have interpreted Jesus's "you" to mean preachers, missionaries, or saints. We superimpose these titles and read the text as "preachers are the light of the world" or "missionaries are the light of the world," but this is an erroneous understanding of the scripture.

In fact, if we are true disciples of Christ, I believe the proper interpretation of the text is to insert each of our names where we see the word "you." "Nicole is the light of the world, Kwame is the light of the world, and Akiri is the light of the world."

If we did this, then we would be more conscious of the fact that every "you" in scripture carries with it a level of tremendous personal responsibility. In part, I think that it is the awareness of this responsibility that causes the church to point the finger at someone else regarding the overwhelming darkness in our world. If we pretend like God isn't talking to us, then we can excuse ourselves from being responsible for doing something about the atrocities in our world. We comfort ourselves by saying that Jesus was only speaking to his apostles, those special twelve who had been handpicked by God to follow Him. But while the twelve were in attendance, Matthew 7:28 says, "The people were astonished," which extends Jesus's call to "you" to include everyone who wholeheartedly calls upon the name of the Lord. It's time that Christians accept God's "you" as a personal call to service.

Secondly, Jesus uses the linking verb "are," which is a present-tense verb meaning that the subject "you" is currently, in its present state, everything that He will reveal later in the verse. Again, examining what Jesus didn't say is important if we are to understand our mission. He didn't say the subject "you" *will be*; He said you *are*. At the time of Jesus's speech, everyone listening to Him was already everything He was going to say to them. They didn't need to wait thirty days, put on sackcloth and ashes, fast, or go to the temple and offer countless sacrifices. Jesus said, "You are," and He is speaking these same two words to each of us who put our trust in Him.

Unfortunately, many of us have been taught, whether purposefully or accidentally, that we have to grow in our faith and reach maturity before we can really be used by God. While I am a proponent of new believers getting a solid foundation in the faith, I also believe that at the moment of our new birth, we have the fullness of Christ. As a result, in our present infantile state, we *are* everything God called us to be, and as we work out our salvation with fear and trembling, our impact will become greater and greater.[5] This maturity doctrine provides a suitable platform for the enemy to subtly prevent us from carrying out Jesus's mandate. Many of us placed our trust in Christ decades ago, and yet we still make excuses such as, "God is still working on me" or "I'm not in a position to push back the darkness in the world because I have my own darkness to fight." But Jesus left no room for these types of cop outs. Jesus didn't qualify his statement by vetting the audience to see who had experience with optics, the study of light. He simply made a statement of fact. Isn't it interesting how we say that we aren't qualified for our assignment, but we are always eager for promotion? We say that we are too inexperienced to serve, but somehow we feel that we are mature enough to be served. Jesus said, "You are," because He is, and that truth should settle every argument that seeks to exalt itself against God's call to every believer.[6]

Next, Jesus chose to use the definite article "the," which distinguishes the word following its use as distinct and set apart. Jesus says you are currently the light—not *a* light, but *the* light. He makes a differentiation between lesser lights and reveals that everyone who places their trust in Him is *the* light. This is important because Paul tells us in 2

Corinthians 11:14–15 that Satan and his ministers masquerade as angels of light. Those who sit in darkness can easily be ensnared by a counterfeit when they don't know what the original looks like. Jesus has called us to reveal Him, the authentic, everlasting, and inextinguishable Light to a dark world. We are not just another light; we are, right now, *the* light.

Again, Jesus's intentional use of this word forces those of us who call ourselves Christians to stop praying for God to change the world. The truth of the matter is that He is waiting on us. Has it ever occurred to us that God is not a micromanager? Once He has empowered us and given us His authority, He expects results. The Light has made us *the* light. God has given us Himself to illuminate a dark world, and the fact that it still remains dark is a result of our negligence and not His indifference. It is interesting to note that the Ghanaian phrase, "Light off," also communicates this truth, in that, the phrase is singular and not plural. "Light off" reveals that there is only one light that has the preeminence but unfortunately, it is currently switched off.

In the beginning, the world was enveloped in darkness, and God said, "Let there be light, and there was light" (Genesis 1:3). Where did this light come from? This light only revealed the Light who had called it forth and in turn eradicated the darkness. Similarly, we are called to reveal the Light who has called us by being *the* light in this world.

So what does it mean to be the light? Light not only reveals what is indiscernible in the dark; it also produces warmth, it heals, and it aids in growth. Jesus tells His hearers that they are the solution to the world's problems of poverty, sickness, loneliness, and stagnation. Believers don't have a solution; we *are* the solution. We are the door of opportunity that an unemployed person needs to get back on their feet. We are the shoulder that the widow needs to cry on. We are the medicine that those in the hospital need to cure them of their ailments. We are the parents to the orphan. We are the food to the hungry. We are the light to those who sit in darkness. I know that this kind of talk makes many Christians uncomfortable because it puts us in a position of responsibility and power that we feel we aren't qualified for. While it's true that we are mere mortals with limitations, the fact still remains that Jesus said, "You are the light of the world." Our inadequacies and human frailties are not up for discussion. We must stop making excuses and shine forth His light.

The last three words, "of," "the," and "world," can be examined together. This is where I believe many of us miss God's intention for making us the light. Jesus reveals that His followers are currently luminaries, but He uses the preposition "of" to answer the question of where we are to shine. Our mandate is to flood the world with light, but far too often we position ourselves within the four walls of the church and attempt to shine in an already-lit atmosphere. A flashlight is unnecessary unless conditions dictate the need for one. To use a flashlight during the day is not only a waste of energy but also a waste of power. Unfortunately, many Christians are willing to be what they think is a light only within the confines of a church building. While there are many ways that we can serve in the church, the fulfillment of our purpose is found in the world.

Oftentimes, Christians become frustrated because no one recognizes their light or talent, and opportunities aren't made for them to shine, but the frustration is a result of shining in the wrong location. Light competes in the midst of other light, but it immediately finds expression in darkness. We will never know the true power that has been invested in us as long as we stay in illuminated atmospheres.

Jesus never intended for us to feed the fed, warm the warmed, or clothe the clothed. He empowered us to light up the darkness. And when we refuse to shine in darkness, we waste energy and power and produce few results for the kingdom of God. As conduits of the light, our purpose for being, the reason for our existence, is to be the light to those who sit in darkness.

Currently, one-fifth of the world's population does not have access to electricity;[7] not coincidentally, these same areas are the least evangelized in the world. Unfortunately, instead of embracing God's "you" as a personal call to action, many Christians sit back and wait for someone else to be the light or seek to outshine their brothers and sisters in Christ. All the while, humanity is forced to wait in frustration as they stumble over their own feet, crying "light off!"

Chapter

"We must work the works of Him who sent Me as long as
it is day; night is coming when no one can work.

—John 9:4 (NASB)

As I continued to seek God for further
understanding, He reminded me of the long, hot, and
restless nights that my family and I endured and of
the three effects of "light off" that I observed.

As I stated previously, the sun sets at around
6:00 p.m. year round, and without the sun as a source
of light, we were in complete darkness. Naturally, we
would light candles, use our solar-powered lamps
(which didn't work well), and our battery-operated
lamps (D batteries are almost impossible to find here)
in an attempt to push back the darkness. Some of our

neighbors were fortunate enough to turn on their generators and fill the night air with the roar and smell of diesel being converted to electricity. Despite these substitutes, nothing could come close to having the real thing. When we wanted to leave one room and go to another, we had to carry the source of light with us because its reach was limited. The quality of light was mediocre at best and could not be sustained without lighting a new candle, putting in new batteries, or purchasing more fuel. Not only that, these quick fixes didn't address our need for cooling both for ourselves and our groceries. These substitutes were not only inferior to electricity, they were, in fact, an additional cost.

Since Christians fail to be the light in the world, people must look for substitutes. As stated previously, Satan and his ministers transform themselves into angels of light and seduce the minds of desperate men and women. Because we have turned our spiritual "light" off, humanity seeks psychics, mediums, and gurus for advice. They attempt to release themselves from emotional and physical pain by ingesting prescription and nonprescription drugs. Looking for fulfillment and purpose, they fill their houses with expensive trinkets and gadgets. Longing to be loved and accepted, they share the most intimate parts of themselves with strangers. This is all done in search for light—the light that we have been called to be in the world.

Like the alternatives to electricity, these desperate attempts at illumination are empty, fleeting, and costly. Proverbs 29:18 makes it very clear that people perish without proper direction and guidance. In a quest for truth, many people resort to counterfeit sources of light because Christians are too busy debating truth with one another or too preoccupied with our own lives to turn the light on. We read the newspaper and condemn the heinous acts of hopeless men and women, but we refuse to light the way. May God convict our hearts and cause us to be a lighthouse leading wayward travelers along life's journey to safe shores.

The second phenomenon that I noticed

during these dark nights was the sudden appearance of ants, spiders, and mosquitos. Although these insects are not uncommon to see during the day in tropical climates, the proliferation of them during "light off" was alarming. No matter where you live in the world, we all know that creepy crawlers come out at night. We have all turned on a light and witnessed roaches scatter or the flick of a rodent's tail as it disappears. We have even entered old, abandoned houses or barns and seen insects crawling freely, even in broad daylight. The lack of consistent light causes these nocturnal creatures to feel comfortable scrounging for food at all times of the day.

I saw this play out in my own house, when the lights were off for multiple days in a row. We could hardly walk into the kitchen or bathroom without dodging an army of ants marching in formation. Furthermore, the insects hardly scurried when we entered the room with a candle or a flashlight because there was limited wattage or power behind those temporary sources of light.

As the body of Christ continues to shine in illuminated places, the forces of darkness have a free-for-all and go unabated. They openly and publically carry out their plans of destruction and are unfazed by lesser lights. They only retreat when *the* light shines and expels them. Demonic forces operate in darkness, and as long as those who have been called out of darkness refuse to reflect His marvelous light, the world will continue to self-destruct.[8] Just as ineffective and unsustainable as candles were to eliminating the darkness that "light off" created in our home, so are the man-made attempts of addressing the ills of society. It is nothing more than the blind leading the blind, but what other options do they have when those who are called to be the light refuse to shine?

Is it possible for believers to sit by and watch laws be passed that defy the mandates of Scripture and destroy the fabric of civilized society without being moved to action? Can followers of Christ remain silent when it becomes easier for children to see violence and hear obscenities through media outlets than it is to hear the Word of God preached? Are our hearts so callous that they remain unbroken for those who still place their trust in idols of wood, hay, and stone? These societal ills cannot be remedied by legislation or well-funded programs. Darkness only responds to the light. So rise and shine, and drive back the forces of darkness in this world.

The last effect of *dumsor* (translated as "off and on") was simply the lack of productivity that occurred. Due to the lack of light, neither we nor the children were able to complete work assignments. No electricity meant that our old laptop, which would only stay charged if it was plugged in, no longer worked. Reading by candlelight is a romantic notion when you have other options, but when it is your only alternative, it becomes less attractive. Our cell phones, iPods, Nintendo DS, and tablets all require electricity if they are not already charged, and multiple days without electricity prevents this from happening. As a result, we would simply just go to bed.

After tossing and turning all night trying to

find a cool spot on the floor and stave off swarms of mosquitos, we would awake in the morning completely exhausted. This resulted in a less-than-productive day at school and work because we were too tired to be excellent. As you can see, it became a cycle—unproductive at home and unproductive at work, all because of "light off." Businesses experienced the same difficulty. Grocery stores were unable to keep their produce and meats refrigerated without electricity, and the cost of fuel to run a generator bankrupted many other businesses.[9] The energy crisis forced many entrepreneurs and companies into a season of idleness. In John 9:4, Jesus reiterates this point when He says that no man can work at night.

When we look at governments around the world and the promises for a better tomorrow for their citizens, we see a lack of productivity. In the United States of America, students have scored well below Asian and European countries on academic assessments. As a result, education reform has been a priority for many decades but with no tangible gains.

The Israeli and Palestinian conflict has been raging for centuries, and there is seemingly no progress. Ghana began transmitting electricity in the 1920s, and almost a hundred years later, there is still inconsistent output across the nation. Growth and advancement are only achieved in the light.

Where are the Christian presidents who wholly follow the Lord? Where are the light bearers in education? Where are the destroyers of darkness in positions of power? Why does Ghana continue to contend with inconsistent electricity when 71 percent of Ghanaians identify themselves as followers of the Light? A country, a city, a home, or a person cannot be productive without the direction, guidance, and fuel that light gives. The answer is looking each of us in the mirror every morning. "You are the light of the world" (Matthew 5:14).

Our inactivity has forced men and women to seek help elsewhere, which only deepens their depravity. The forces of darkness go uncontested and drag countless souls to hell because we refuse to flip the light switch on. The world spins its wheels without advancing or progressing because those of us with the answers won't go where the questions are being asked. Change will only come when believers in the Lord Jesus Christ decide to turn their light on and transmit the power of the cross in a dark world.

Chapter

"Therefore do not be partakers with them; for you were
formerly darkness, but now you are Light in the Lord; walk
as children of Light."

—Ephesians 5:7–8 (NASB)

Now that I better understood what God
revealed in Matthew 5:14 and how my refusal to be
the light affected the world, I set out to discover the
reasons for Ghana's energy crisis and how they relate
to our inability as Christians to consistently reveal
God to a dying world.

Let me begin by confessing that I am not a
historian nor do I have a keen interest in
sociopolitical genealogies of foreign countries.
Nevertheless, in order for me to fully grasp what the

Holy Spirit was teaching me, I set out to understand how Ghana's electricity issues began. My research led me to three sources of the phenomenon called "light off."

The first reason that Ghana's citizens experience *dumsor* is the temperamental nature of its primary source of electricity. Ghana generates approximately 70 percent of its electricity from hydroelectric dams operated by the Volta River Authority.[10] In order to supply twenty-six million citizens with consistent electricity, water levels must remain high. This water is primarily gathered from annual rainfall. Unfortunately, Ghana's rainfall has been below average for the past several years, thus diminishing the water levels and subsequently the output of electricity. Water levels must be maintained in order for all six turbines that generate electricity at the Akosombo Dam to remain in operation. In the last few months, a request was made to the government by the VRA to shut down three turbines due to the lack of rainfall in the north.[11] If all six turbines remain operational when water levels are low, it can cause severe mechanical issues.

In like manner, our ability to be the light is in direct proportion to remaining connected to our Source. We can only be the light when we are abiding in the Light. Too often, Christians have made professions of faith and then returned to life as usual. Jesus's audience on the Mount of Olives was in possession of the light that could change the world, but once they left the mountain, it was their responsibility to remain plugged into the Source of their light. In the natural realm, a lack of consistent rain prevents hydroelectric turbines from producing consistent electricity. In the spirit realm, a lack of *reign* prevents Christians from revealing truth, producing growth, and eradicating darkness. To call Jesus "Lord" and at the same time refuse to follow His instructions is a paradox. Either He reigns in our lives, or He doesn't. The evidence of His reign is characterized by our production of light. If people and circumstances around us aren't growing, receiving direction, or producing change, then we need to check our spiritual water levels. I believe if consistent and abundant rain fell, Ghana's energy crisis could improve. Likewise, if followers of Jesus allowed Christ to reign in their lives, they could light up the world.

The second cause of "light off" is the antiquated machinery that was built fifty years ago and that has not received adequate maintenance. Ghana's largest producer of hydroelectric power is the Akosombo Dam, which was erected in 1965 under the leadership of Ghana's first president, Kwame Nkrumah.[12] After only a few years of growth and expansion, the dam was unable to adequately supply the needs of Ghana's citizens. Nevertheless, it wasn't until 1981, after the demand had reached critical levels, that the Kpong Dam was built to help meet the growing demand of Ghana's economy. It would take another thirty years for the Bui Dam to be built in northern Ghana to help supply electricity to that area and to offset the load carried by the other two dams.

Someone may read this and think that these

projects are a sign of progress and advancement, but these dams were built out of sheer necessity. These structures were erected after the country was already in a state of crisis. Instead of being proactive and anticipating the future demands and servicing the existing infrastructure, officials waited until the situation reached the point of no return.

Furthermore, Ghana also produces limited amounts of electricity from thermal plants, but most of these plants are currently undergoing much-needed repairs. Due to their overdue maintenance, they are unable to help ease the current demand of power.

If rainwater is the source of the electricity and the dam is the structure that converts the rain into energy, then God reigning in our lives produces the light, and we are the structure that converts that light into good works in the world. It is our responsibility to be proactive in servicing the channels by which God uses to disseminate light. If we don't attend to our relationship with the Lord, but rather allow it to become old, stagnant, and fractured, then we will not be able to keep up with the demand.

I believe that this is one of the main reasons that Christians are failing to light up a dark world. Many of us have neglected our first love and sought fame, glory, and positions of prominence. In our quest to be used by God, we have replaced our quiet times with ministry preparations. Without drawing from our Source on a daily basis, our output is limited at best. The darkness that we are called to eliminate has reached unprecedented levels that we are not equipped to handle because we have gone too long without proper spiritual maintenance. Confessing our sins, seeking God through prayer, studying His Word, and engaging in consistent Christian fellowship is how we ensure that our "structures" remain sound. Allowing sin to go unconfessed leads to spiritual erosion and decay. It is imperative that we take time to examine our hearts on a daily basis and ask the Holy Spirit to point out areas in our lives that need immediate repair. It will be too late if we wait to get connected to our Source until we face a difficult challenge that requires concentrated amounts of light.

We must be servicing our relationship continually, anticipating that there is a mounting darkness that refuses to be expelled except by the arrival of true light.

The third culprit in Ghana's energy crisis is the country's decision to provide electricity to neighboring countries. Currently, Togo and Benin receive some electricity from Ghana's crippled energy sector. It seems irrational to export electricity when you cannot produce sufficient amounts for your own citizens, but this is the current reality in Ghana. In fact, in recent months, Benin and Togo sent a delegation to Ghana to ask for more than the fifty megawatts a week that they currently receive.[13] In an effort to save face, officials have assured these neighboring countries that as Ghana's output increases, they in turn will increase export amounts. This desire to align with neighboring countries and share resources is counterproductive. 1 Timothy 3:4 speaks of an overseer being responsible to manage his own house well before he leads in God's house.

As light bearers, we cannot give what we do not have. It's true that Jesus said in Matthew 5:14, "You are the light of the world." But *that* light must be fueled and maintained by *the* Light. If we have not filled our lamps with oil, then it's useless to offer to illuminate our neighbors' path. Our power comes from the Omnipotent One, and without staying connected to Him, we have nothing to offer anyone else. Furthermore, we are called to be the light of the world in our particular sphere of influence. If we are teachers, then we are called to light up our classrooms. If we are mechanics, then we are anointed to push back the darkness in the lives of our customers. If we are stay-at-home mothers, then we are empowered to illuminate our families. Jesus's mandate to change the world starts right where we are and possibly, in time, includes the world at large. In an effort to be noble, we can attempt to help people in an area in which we ourselves are in need of help. Lighting up the world where we currently live, work, and play produces far greater results than providing inconsistent light to a multitude.

Relying on one major source of electricity, failing to provide timely maintenance, and exporting power that we can't afford are some of the factors that contribute to Ghana's energy crisis. Likewise, refraining from consistent daily fellowship with our Source, failing to address the sins in our lives, and seeking to minister to people outside of our sphere of influence all lead to the spiritual condition called "light off."

By no means is this an exhaustive list of the underlying factors that contribute to Ghana's current energy crisis, nor is it a thorough examination of the problem. But it's a start that can help each of us take stock of our own limited output of light and reconnect to our Source.

Chapter

> "Let your light shine before men in such a way that they may see your good works, and glorify your Father who is in heaven."
>
> —Matthew 5:16 (NASB)

The last words that the Holy Spirit spoke to me became a challenge of sorts. He said, "Every time that the lights go off, turn your light on." I wasn't sure what He meant by those words, but I was willing to do anything other than call ECG and work myself up into a frustrated frenzy. I decided that the best way that I could be the light was to begin to pray and intercede for those who sat in darkness, both naturally and spiritually. I must admit that sometimes I didn't want to pray, and so I didn't. There were times that I felt pity for myself and cried instead of prayed.

Despite these moments of weakness, there were also times that I channeled my frustration into bold and fervent prayers. I may never know how those prayers brought illumination to countless souls, but I am sure that they availed much, in accordance with James 5:16.

So did I only pray about being the light when the lights were off? Of course not, because spiritual darkness is prevalent and pervasive and is not eradicated by physical light. So when the lights were on naturally, I also prayed and sought opportunities to be the light in my sphere of influence. I began with sharing these truths with my children, who watched their missionary mother struggle with a call that I already thought I had answered by virtue of the fact that I was living in Ghana. I was able to model for my children the daily application of scriptures like Philippians 4:11–13, which speaks of being content in every situation because of Christ's strength within me.

I am convinced that every second of every minute, every minute of every hour, and every hour of every day, there is some soul in need of spiritual illumination, and therefore, every Christian should be engaged in the lighting business. I am an educator by profession, and I believe that God has called each of us through our natural careers to produce growth and provide direction to the world. Mounting a pulpit or standing before thousands is the call of a few, but each of us has been called to be the light of the world.

We can no longer be satisfied with emitting light when we choose to or when it is convenient, any more than a government can continue to transmit limited supply of electricity to its citizens while they live in well-lit homes. Followers of Christ must refrain from engaging in the phenomenon called *dumsor* (off and on) and instead become consistent carriers of the light for the glory of the Light.

So what can we do to be the light? Look around your sphere of influence, and meet the needs there, first. Is there a single mom in your neighborhood? Does your local school board need Christian voices on the panel? Are there homeless people along your daily route to work? Do your children's friends need a safe place to hang out after school? Are there orphans living in abandoned buildings across the street? Does your place of employment need organization and vision? The beauty of Jesus's call is that it is tailor-made for each of us. We are not required to shine like anyone else; we are free to chase darkness by any means necessary.

The Holy Spirit challenged me, and now I challenge you. Take ownership of Jesus's "you," and right now, where you are, decide to be the light to those who sit in darkness in your sphere of influence. Refuse to keep another soul frustrated, crying, "light off," because they are waiting for you to shine the light in the dark situations of their life. Although Ghanaians coined the term "light off,' its effects can be felt worldwide. It is my prayer that the phrase "light on" sweeps across the globe as believers obey the command of Jesus and become the light of the world.

"For so the Lord has commanded us, 'I have placed you as a light before the Gentiles, that you may bring salvation to the end of the earth.'"

—Acts 13:47 (NASB)

Notes

[i] "26.4 million Ghanaian citizens," *The World Bank Group 2015*, accessed September 23, 2015, http://data.worldbank.org/country/ghana.

[2] "Carrying my cross," Matthew 16:24, New American Standard Bible.

[3] : "Electricity Sector in Ghana," *Wikipedia,* accessed August 29, 2015, https://en.wikipedia.org/wiki/Electricity_sector_in_ Ghana.

[4] "Laissez-faire" is the policy of leaving things to take their own course, without interfering, Merriam-Webster, accessed November 2, 2015, http://www.merriam-webster.com/dictionary/laissez-faire

[5] "Work out your salvation with fear and trembling," Philippians 2:12, New American Standard Bible.

[6] "Every argument that seeks to exalt itself," 2 Corinthians 10:5, New American Standard Bible.

[7] "Blackout," B. Walsh, *Time Magazine,* last modified September 15, 2013, accessed September 22, 2015, http://business.time.com/2013/09/15/Blackout-1-Billion-Live-Without-Electric-Light/.

[8] "Called out of darkness into marvelous light," 1 Peter 2:9, New American Standard Bible.

[9] : "Dumsor Collapsed Business," *The Pulse*, last modified April 10, 2015, accessed September 22, 2015, http://pulse.com.gh/news/dumsor-collapse-business-dumsor-caused-ghana-nearly-ghc1b-in-2014-isser-id3644532.html.

[10] "Electricity Sector in Ghana," *Wikipedia,* last modified August 29, 2015, accessed September 20, 2015, https://en.wikipedia.org/wiki/Electricity_sector_in_Ghana.

[11] Akosombo to Shut down 3 more Turbines,"
Citifmonline, last modified July 23, 2015, accessed
September 21, 2015,
http://citifmonline.com/2015/07/23/more-dumsor-
akosombo-dam-to-shut-down-3-more-
turbines/#sthash.vtiokwuldpuf.

[12] "History of Akosombo Dam," *Ministry of Petroleum,*
last modified May 8, 2011, accessed September 22,
2015, http://www.energymin.gov.gh/?p=1146.

[13] "Benin, Togo ask Ghana for more Power," *Joy
Online,* last modified March 2, 2015, accessed
September 22, 2015,
http://business.myjoyonline.com/pages/news/20130
3/102189.php.

About the Author

Nicole Darko is an ordained minister who has embarked on global missions for almost two decades. She holds a bachelor's degree in speech, an MEd in middle grades language arts, and an education specialist degree in curriculum and instruction.

Her educational training, as well as her ten years of teaching experience, ultimately prepared her to communicate God's word in a way that reaches people of all ages and backgrounds. Nicole's passion and approachable manner make her a highly sought after speaker and presenter.

Darko and her husband Prince were associate ministers at Kingdom Impact Global Ministries in Fayetteville, North Carolina, before moving with their two children to Ghana, West Africa. This experience prompted Darko to write her inspirational debut, *Light Off*.

If you are interested in joining the *Light On* Movement, booking a speaking engagement or obtaining additional copies of this book, please visit www.nicoledarko.com or connect with Nicole via Facebook at www.facebook.com/nicoledarko, and Twitter @NicoleDarko.

www.ingramcontent.com/pod-product-compliance
Lightning Source LLC
Chambersburg PA
CBHW050955050426
42337CB00051B/1254